Shadows of the Past

Shadows of the Past

Stephen Wright

CONTENTS

1

The Nature of Hauntings

Defining Hauntings

Hauntings, as a phenomenon, have captivated human imagination for centuries, manifesting in various forms across different cultures. At their core, hauntings are typically defined as occurrences where a spirit or ghost is believed to be present in a particular location, often tied to a significant event or individual from the past. These manifestations can take many shapes, ranging from auditory phenomena like whispers or footsteps to visual apparitions that may appear as shadowy figures or fully formed entities. The complexity of hauntings lies in their ability to evoke emotional responses, intertwining the realms of the living and the deceased.

Historically, hauntings are often linked to specific locations, such as battlefields, old homes, or abandoned buildings. Many cultures have developed a rich tapestry of urban legends surrounding these sites, suggesting that the energies of past events linger in the environment. For example, numerous castles across Europe are said to be haunted by the spirits of former residents who met untimely ends. These narratives not only serve to entertain but also act as a window into the societal beliefs of the time, highlighting how the living make sense of grief, trauma, and unresolved issues through the lens of the supernatural.

The investigation of hauntings has evolved significantly over the years, with a growing interest in the methods used to explore these phenomena. Paranormal investigations often employ a variety of tools, ranging from traditional mediums to modern ghost hunting equipment like electromagnetic field meters and infrared cameras. These tools aim to detect anomalies that may indicate a ghostly presence, allowing enthusiasts to gather evidence and share their findings within the community. The rise of technology in ghost hunting has also led to a more scientific approach, encouraging a critical examination of the evidence collected and fostering discussions about the validity and interpretation of such experiences.

Celebrity ghost encounters have played a unique role in shaping public perception of hauntings. Stories of famous figures encountering spirits or visiting haunted sites often garner significant media attention, leading to increased interest in specific locations. These narratives can elevate the status of a place, transforming it into a tourist attraction while simultaneously reinforcing the belief in the supernatural. For many, the allure of exploring the unknown becomes intertwined with the legacy of well-known personalities, creating a blend of history and myth that continues to intrigue ghost story fans.

Ultimately, defining hauntings requires an understanding of the broader cultural and historical contexts in which they arise. Ghostly manifestations are not merely isolated incidents; they are reflections of collective fears, hopes, and the human desire to connect with those who have passed. As we delve into the shadows of the past, it becomes clear that hauntings serve as more than just eerie tales; they are narratives that connect us to our history, reminding us of the fragility of life and the enduring nature of the human spirit.

Types of Hauntings

Types of hauntings can vary dramatically, each with its unique characteristics and implications. Understanding these different types can enhance the experience of paranormal enthusiasts and provide context for ghost stories that have been passed down through generations. Broadly, hauntings can be categorized into three main types: residual hauntings, intelligent hauntings, and poltergeist activity. Each type reveals distinct narratives surrounding the supernatural, making them essential to the study of ghostly phenomena.

Residual hauntings are often described as imprints of the past, where events replay themselves like a film on a loop. These hauntings typically involve no interaction with the living, as the spirits involved are not aware of their surroundings. They may manifest through sounds, sights, or even scents, often tied to specific locations where the original events took place. Historical locations, such as battlefields or old mansions, are prime examples where residual energy can be felt, creating a captivating backdrop for ghost hunters seeking to capture evidence of the past.

In contrast, intelligent hauntings involve spirits that are aware of their surroundings and can interact with the living. These entities may seek to communicate with those who remain behind, often conveying messages or emotions related to their unfinished business. This type of haunting can be particularly engaging for paranormal investigators, as it provides opportunities for establishing connections through various methods, such as EVP sessions or the use of spirit boards. The narratives surrounding intelligent hauntings often intertwine with personal stories, adding depth to the ghostly encounters that many enthusiasts cherish.

Poltergeist activity is perhaps the most dynamic and often chaotic type of haunting. Unlike residual or intelligent hauntings, poltergeists are characterized by physical disturbances, such as objects being moved, loud noises, or even physical harm. These manifestations are typically linked to a specific individual, often a teenager or someone experiencing emotional turmoil. The phenomenon raises questions about the nature of the disturbances, leading some researchers to consider whether these activities stem from repressed emotions projected into the environment rather than a traditional spirit presence. This type of haunting challenges the boundaries of what is considered a ghostly encounter.

Finally, within each of these categories, there exists a rich tapestry of urban legends and cultural beliefs that shape the understanding of hauntings across different societies. From the ghostly apparitions of famous figures to the chilling stories that circulate in local folklore, these narratives contribute to the allure of ghost hunting. As paranormal enthusiasts continue to explore the realms of the supernatural, the types of hauntings they encounter will not only deepen their appreciation for ghost stories but also enrich their understanding of the historical contexts that give rise to these spectral manifestations.

Cultural Perspectives on Ghosts

Cultural perspectives on ghosts provide a fascinating lens through which we can examine the beliefs, fears, and traditions that have shaped human societies throughout history. Across various cultures, ghostly manifestations are often linked to the unresolved issues of the deceased, reflecting local customs surrounding death, mourning, and the afterlife. In many Asian cultures, for example, the concept of ancestor worship plays a pivotal role, where ghosts are seen as integral to familial continuity. This perspective emphasizes the importance of honoring the dead through rituals that ensure their comfort and prevent them from becoming restless spirits.

In contrast, Western cultures often depict ghosts as eerie figures that haunt specific locations, typically tied to a traumatic event or an untimely death. The narrative of the vengeful or sorrowful ghost is prevalent, with stories emphasizing the need for resolution and closure. This can be seen in the classic ghost story trope of a spirit haunting its former home, seeking justice or closure for past grievances. Such narratives not only entertain but also serve as cautionary tales, encouraging audiences to reflect on their own lives and the impact of unresolved conflicts.

Indigenous cultures worldwide offer diverse interpretations of the spirit world, often viewing ghosts as messengers or guides rather than malevolent entities. For example, many Native American tribes believe in the presence of spirit guides that help the living navigate their journeys. This belief system fosters a respectful relationship with the spirit world, where communication is sought through rituals and ceremonies. Such practices highlight the idea that ghosts can play a constructive role in the lives of the living, facilitating spiritual growth and understanding.

Literature and popular media have also shaped cultural perspectives on ghosts, often reinforcing or challenging traditional beliefs. From Shakespeare's "Hamlet," where the ghost serves as a catalyst for revenge, to contemporary films that explore the psychological implications of hauntings, these narratives reflect society's evolving understanding of death and the afterlife. The portrayal of ghosts in literature often mirrors prevailing societal fears and hopes, serving as a barometer for cultural attitudes toward mortality and the unknown.

As paranormal enthusiasts and ghost story fans delve into these cultural perspectives, they enrich their understanding of the spectral phenomena that have captivated human imagination for centuries. Engaging with the diverse beliefs surrounding ghosts not only enhances the appreciation of ghost stories but also invites deeper reflections on the human condition. By exploring how various cultures interpret and interact with the spirit realm, enthusiasts can uncover a tapestry of beliefs that illustrates the universal quest for meaning and connection beyond the grave.

2

Historical Hauntings

The Ghosts of Ancient Civilizations

The echoes of ancient civilizations linger in the shadows of our modern world, often manifesting as ghostly apparitions, eerie sounds, and inexplicable phenomena. These spectral presences are believed to be remnants of the past, tethered to the sites of their former lives. From the majestic ruins of Rome to the forgotten temples of the Maya, each location has its own stories of hauntings that reflect the cultures that once thrived there. For paranormal enthusiasts, exploring these sites offers a unique opportunity to connect with history while engaging with the unexplained.

One of the most notable examples is the haunting of the Colosseum in Rome, where the spirits of gladiators are said to roam. This iconic arena, once a stage for brutal spectacles, is now a site of reflection on the cruelty of ancient entertainment. Visitors often report feeling a sudden chill or hearing faint whispers that seem to echo the cries of the fallen. The combination of history and the supernatural creates a powerful atmosphere, drawing ghost hunters and historians alike to investigate the spectral activity that surrounds this iconic landmark.

Similarly, the ancient city of Pompeii, buried in ash by the eruption of Mount Vesuvius, holds a tragic yet fascinating narrative. The preserved remains of its inhabitants serve as a poignant reminder of sudden loss. Paranormal investigators have documented numerous encounters with disembodied voices and fleeting shadows, suggesting that the spirits of those who perished may be trapped in the remnants of their former lives. The juxtaposition of beauty and tragedy in Pompeii makes it a compelling site for those interested in the ghostly manifestations of history.

In the Americas, the ancient ruins of the Maya civilization are steeped in legends of hauntings tied to their rich spiritual beliefs. Sites such as Chichen Itza and Tikal are not only archaeological wonders but also hotbeds of paranormal activity. Reports of orbs, strange lights, and even apparitions resembling ancient priests have captivated ghost story fans and researchers alike. These encounters highlight a continued connection to the spiritual practices of the past, as the Maya believed in the cyclical nature of life and death, where the spirits of their ancestors play an integral role in their existence.

Exploring the ghosts of ancient civilizations is not merely an exercise in curiosity; it serves as a bridge between the past and the present. The stories of the dead remind us of the lives once lived and the cultures that shaped our world. For those who engage in spiritualism and mediumship, these sites offer a profound connection to the energies of yesteryear, allowing for communication with those who have long since departed. The reflections on history through paranormal encounters not only enrich our understanding of ancient peoples but also reinforce the idea that, perhaps, their spirits continue to wander, seeking recognition and remembrance in the shadows of time.

Notable Historical Hauntings

Notable historical hauntings often serve as gateways into the past, revealing not only the spectral tales associated with specific locations but also the cultural and social contexts in which these events occurred. One of the most recognized haunted sites is the Tower of London, with its grim history dating back to the Norman Conquest. This fortress has witnessed countless executions, imprisonments, and tragic tales, leading many to believe it is a hotspot for ghostly encounters. Visitors and staff have reported sightings of Anne Boleyn, who was executed in 1536, often described as a headless apparition walking the grounds. Such encounters highlight the enduring impact of historical figures and events on the collective consciousness and the haunting narratives that emerge from them.

Another notable haunting is that of the Myrtles Plantation in Louisiana, which is often referred to as one of America's most haunted homes. Built in the late 18th century, the plantation's history is marred by tales of tragedy, including the alleged murder of a slave named Chloe. Visitors have claimed to see her ghost wandering the grounds, and there are reports of mysterious handprints appearing on mirrors. The plantation's rich history intertwined with the lives of enslaved people underscores the complexities of hauntings that stem from socio-historical injustices. The Myrtles serves as a reminder of how the past can manifest in eerie ways, inviting those interested in the paranormal to explore deeper connections between history and hauntings.

The Eastern State Penitentiary in Philadelphia is another location steeped in haunting lore. Opened in 1829, this prison was known for its radical approach to incarceration, which emphasized solitude and reflection. However, the harsh conditions led to significant psychological distress among inmates, many of whom have been reported as restless spirits. Paranormal investigators frequently cite experiences of cold spots, disembodied voices, and shadowy figures throughout the dilapidated structure. The penitentiary's historical significance and the tragic fates of its inmates create a compelling narrative that entices ghost hunters and history buffs alike, demonstrating how the architectural remnants of the past can become vessels for spectral stories.

In the realm of celebrity encounters with the supernatural, the Winchester Mystery House in San Jose, California, stands out. Built by Sarah Winchester, the widow of firearm magnate William Wirt Winchester, this sprawling mansion is infamous for its architectural oddities and constant renovations. Legend has it that Sarah believed she was haunted by the spirits of those killed by Winchester rifles, prompting her to construct a labyrinthine structure that would confuse these spirits. Today, visitors report inexplicable phenomena, such as sudden changes in temperature and the sensation of being watched. This connection between a historical figure and her haunted legacy illustrates the intersection of fame, tragedy, and the paranormal.

Lastly, the haunting of Gettysburg, Pennsylvania, offers a poignant reflection on the impact of war and loss. As the site of one of the Civil War's bloodiest battles, Gettysburg is often described as a spiritual battleground. Ghostly manifestations, including apparitions of soldiers and eerie sounds of battle, have been reported by both visitors and paranormal investigators. The town's historical significance as a marker of sacrifice and valor creates a palpable sense of presence, inviting exploration into the emotional weight carried by such sites. The hauntings at Gettysburg serve as reminders of the unresolved traumas of history, providing a rich tapestry for those fascinated by the intertwining of the past and the paranormal.

The Influence of History on Ghost Stories

The history of ghost stories is deeply intertwined with the cultural, social, and political contexts of the times in which they were told. Each era has its own unique fears, beliefs, and societal norms that shape the narratives surrounding hauntings. From ancient civilizations to modern urban legends, the evolution of ghost stories reflects humanity's ongoing fascination with life after death and the unknown. Understanding this relationship between history and ghostly tales allows paranormal enthusiasts to appreciate the deeper meanings behind the hauntings they investigate.

In ancient cultures, ghost stories often served as cautionary tales, providing moral lessons or explaining natural phenomena. For instance, the ghostly apparitions of the ancient Greeks were frequently linked to the gods and the afterlife, reflecting their beliefs about morality and divine retribution. In medieval Europe, the rise of Christianity transformed the perception of spirits, framing them as either angels or demons. This shift influenced ghost stories, which began to emphasize the moral consequences of earthly actions, often featuring restless souls seeking redemption or vengeance. These historical contexts not only informed the stories themselves but also shaped the cultural practices surrounding death and the afterlife.

As societies progressed, the Industrial Revolution introduced new anxieties and existential questions, leading to a resurgence of interest in spiritualism and the supernatural. The rapid changes in technology and urbanization created a sense of dislocation, prompting people to seek solace in the idea of communication with the dead. This period saw the rise of mediums and ghost-hunting practices, as well as a proliferation of ghost stories that resonated with the fears and hopes of the time. Historical hauntings began to be framed as reflections of societal trauma and loss, often connected to the upheaval experienced by individuals and communities during this transformative period.

In contemporary times, ghost stories continue to evolve, influenced by modern technology and popular culture. The advent of the internet has facilitated the sharing of urban legends and personal ghost encounters, creating a global tapestry of haunting narratives. Television shows and films have also played a significant role in shaping perceptions of the paranormal, often drawing from historical contexts to craft compelling narratives. Ghost hunting has transformed into a popular hobby, complete with specialized equipment and a community of enthusiasts eager to explore the mysteries of the past. As a result, modern ghost stories often blend historical elements with contemporary experiences, reflecting a continuing dialogue between the living and the dead.

The influence of history on ghost stories is not merely a matter of context; it is a dynamic interplay that enriches our understanding of the supernatural. Each ghostly tale serves as a vessel through which the past communicates with the present, offering insights into the fears, hopes, and values of different eras. For paranormal enthusiasts and ghost story fans, exploring these historical influences enhances the experience of ghost hunting and storytelling, revealing the layered meanings within each haunting. By examining the historical roots of ghost stories, we can uncover the timeless themes that resonate across generations, affirming our collective fascination with the unknown and the enduring presence of shadows from the past.

3 |

Urban Legends and Ghost Stories

Origins of Urban Legends

Urban legends have long captivated the imagination, serving as a bridge between folklore and contemporary culture. These tales often emerge from a mixture of historical events, cultural anxieties, and communal storytelling, reflecting societal fears and values. Their origins can frequently be traced back to real incidents that have undergone a transformation through retelling, embellishment, and reinterpretation. This process allows urban legends to evolve, adapting to the times while maintaining a core element of intrigue that keeps them alive in the collective consciousness.

One of the key factors in the inception of urban legends is the role of oral tradition. Before the widespread availability of mass media, stories were transmitted through word of mouth, often changing as they passed from person to person. This fluidity allowed for the incorporation of local color, personal experience, and contemporary issues, making each retelling unique. As a result, urban legends often reflect the cultural and social landscapes of the times in which they are told, evolving alongside societal changes and technological advancements.

Another significant influence on urban legends is the media, particularly in the modern era. Newspapers, television, and the internet have played crucial roles in shaping and disseminating these stories. High-profile crimes, unexplained phenomena, and sensationalized news reports can give rise to legends that capture public attention. The virality of social media has further accelerated this process, enabling urban legends to spread quickly and reach diverse audiences, often becoming part of a shared cultural experience. This intersection of media and folklore not only amplifies existing legends but also inspires new ones, as people creatively adapt and reinterpret narratives to suit their own contexts.

Psychological factors also contribute to the formation of urban legends. These stories often tap into common fears and anxieties, such as fears of the unknown, mistrust of authority, or concerns about safety. By embodying these fears in narrative form, urban legends become a way for individuals and communities to process and confront their anxieties. They serve as cautionary tales, moral lessons, or simply entertainment, allowing people to explore the darker aspects of human experience in a safe and controlled manner. The allure of the unknown, combined with the thrill of fear, ensures that urban legends remain compelling and relevant.

The connection between urban legends and historical hauntings cannot be overlooked. Many urban legends have roots in historical events or figures, transforming real-life tragedies into ghost stories that linger in the public imagination.

Locations associated with these legends often become sites of paranormal interest, attracting ghost hunters and enthusiasts eager to uncover the truth behind the tales. By examining the origins of urban legends, paranormal investigators can gain insights into the cultural and historical contexts that shape these narratives, enriching their understanding of the haunting phenomena and the ghosts that inhabit our collective memories.

Iconic Ghost Stories from Around the World

Ghost stories have always captivated audiences, transcending cultures and generations. They serve as a reflection of societal fears, historical events, and cultural beliefs. From the chilling tales of haunted castles in Europe to the eerie legends of restless spirits in Asia, these stories resonate with the human experience of loss, love, and the unknown. Each region boasts its own iconic ghost stories, steeped in history and rich in detail, making them essential components of global folklore.

One of the most famous ghost stories originates from Scotland, where the legend of the Grey Lady of Stirling Castle continues to intrigue both locals and visitors. This spectral figure is said to be the ghost of Lady Anne, who tragically lost her life in the castle. Sightings of the Grey Lady have been reported for centuries, with witnesses describing her as a sorrowful figure wandering the halls, often seen near the castle's chapel. The story not only captures the imagination but also highlights the intertwining of history and the supernatural, as Stirling Castle has played a significant role in Scotland's turbulent past.

In Japan, the tale of the Yūrei presents a culturally significant take on ghostly encounters. These spirits are believed to be the souls of individuals who died in a state of emotional turmoil or without proper funeral rites. The story of Okiku, a servant girl wrongfully accused of theft, illustrates the haunting nature of the Yūrei. After her death, Okiku's spirit is said to have returned to haunt her master, counting dishes as a symbol of her unresolved grievances. This narrative not only captivates but also reflects the cultural importance of honor and justice within Japanese society, providing a unique perspective on ghostly manifestations.

Moving to the Americas, the legend of La Llorona, or the Weeping Woman, is a haunting tale that has echoed through generations. Said to be the spirit of a woman who drowned her children in a fit of rage and now roams riverbanks weeping for her lost offspring, La Llorona serves as a cautionary tale. The legend has numerous variations across Mexico and Latin American countries, but the core theme remains the same: a tragic figure consumed by sorrow, warning others against the consequences of their actions. This story not only serves as a ghostly warning but also reflects broader themes of motherhood, loss, and regret in the cultural psyche.

These iconic ghost stories are more than mere entertainment; they are historical narratives that reveal much about the cultures from which they originate. They intertwine with local legends, social customs, and collective memories, creating a rich tapestry of human experience. For paranormal enthusiasts and ghost story fans, these tales offer a glimpse into the past, inviting exploration and investigation. Each story serves as a reminder of the enduring power of folklore to convey moral lessons, cultural values, and the human longing for connection, even beyond the veil of death.

The Role of Urban Legends in Modern Haunting Tales

Urban legends have long served as the backbone of modern ghost stories, bridging the gap between folklore and contemporary hauntings. These narratives, often rooted in cultural fears and societal anxieties, provide a fertile ground for the supernatural. They evolve as they are passed down through generations, reflecting the values and concerns of the times. In the context of hauntings, urban legends not only entertain but also serve as cautionary tales, warning individuals about the consequences of certain actions or the dangers lurking in familiar spaces.

The role of urban legends in shaping ghost stories is particularly significant as they often draw upon real locations and historical events. This connection adds a layer of authenticity that resonates with paranormal enthusiasts, who are drawn to the idea that a haunting might have a basis in reality. Locations like abandoned hospitals, old schools, and historic homes become the settings for these tales, allowing urban legends to intertwine with documented history. The allure of exploring these sites is amplified by the belief that lingering spirits may still inhabit them, rooted in the narratives that have been spun around them.

Moreover, urban legends often reflect collective fears and societal issues, making them particularly relevant in times of crisis. For example, tales of haunted urban spaces can mirror anxieties about urban decay, crime, or loss of community. These stories serve as a coping mechanism for individuals grappling with their fears, allowing them to confront the unknown through the lens of story-telling. As new legends emerge, they often incorporate modern technology and social dynamics, evolving to remain pertinent to contemporary audiences. This adaptability ensures that urban legends continue to thrive in the realm of hauntings.

In the realm of paranormal investigations, urban legends provide a roadmap for ghost hunters.

Many enthusiasts seek out the sites connected to these tales, armed with various ghost hunting equipment to capture evidence of the supernatural. The legends inform the methodology of these investigations, as the stories often highlight specific phenomena, such as apparitions or unexplained sounds. This intersection of folklore and technology creates a unique dynamic, as investigators attempt to validate the legends through empirical means while remaining open to the mysteries that may defy explanation.

Lastly, the impact of urban legends extends beyond individual encounters; they shape the cultural landscape of ghostly manifestations in literature and media. Authors and filmmakers often draw inspiration from these tales, weaving them into narratives that explore the complexities of fear, loss, and the afterlife. This blend of history, legend, and fiction creates a rich tapestry that captivates audiences and perpetuates the cycle of storytelling. As urban legends continue to evolve, they will undoubtedly remain a vital component in the ongoing dialogue about hauntings, ensuring that the shadows of the past continue to influence the present.

4

Paranormal Investigations

The Evolution of Paranormal Investigation

The practice of paranormal investigation has undergone significant transformation since its inception, evolving from folklore and superstition into a structured field of inquiry. In ancient cultures, phenomena such as ghostly apparitions and otherworldly encounters were often attributed to deities or spirits, with shamans and priests serving as intermediaries between the living and the supernatural. These early interpretations laid the groundwork for understanding hauntings, as they provided a framework for explaining the unexplainable through the lens of spirituality and belief systems. The narratives that emerged from these encounters were deeply intertwined with cultural identities, shaping local legends and ghost stories that have persisted through generations.

With the advent of the Enlightenment in the 17th and 18th centuries, the approach to the supernatural began to shift. Rationalism and scientific inquiry took center stage, leading to skepticism about traditional beliefs in ghosts and spirits. However, this period also saw the rise of spiritualism in the 19th century, which combined scientific curiosity with a renewed interest in the afterlife. Mediums, séances, and the first ghost hunting societies emerged during this time, as individuals sought to communicate with the deceased. This blend of science and mysticism sparked public fascination, ultimately paving the way for more systematic paranormal investigations that sought to document and validate experiences through observation and experimentation.

The 20th century marked a pivotal moment in paranormal investigation, as technological advancements began to play a crucial role in the field. The invention of devices such as the electromagnetic field (EMF) meter, digital voice recorders, and infrared cameras enabled investigators to capture evidence of hauntings in ways that were previously unimaginable. These tools allowed enthusiasts to venture into notoriously haunted locations with the hope of gathering scientific data to support their claims. The emergence of television shows dedicated to ghost hunting further popularized the field, showcasing dramatic investigations and encouraging a new wave of interest among the public.

As the 21st century unfolded, paranormal investigation became more accessible to the average person, thanks to the internet and social media. Online forums and communities formed, where enthusiasts could share experiences, theories, and findings. The rise of ghost hunting equipment reviews provided newcomers with guidance on tools that could enhance their investigations. Celebrity ghost encounters also gained traction, further blending the lines between entertainment and genuine inquiry into the paranormal. This democratization of ghost hunting fostered a diverse array of perspectives and methodologies, inviting a wider audience to engage with the mysteries of the afterlife.

Today, the evolution of paranormal investigation continues, characterized by an ongoing dialogue between scientific inquiry and personal belief. Investigators are increasingly incorporating psychological and sociological frameworks into their work, examining the impact of human perception on ghostly experiences. Moreover, the resurgence of interest in historical hauntings and urban legends serves to connect past narratives with present experiences. Paranormal enthusiasts now navigate a rich tapestry of stories and evidence, seeking to understand not only the nature of hauntings but also their place within the broader context of human experience and cultural history.

Notable Paranormal Investigation Techniques

Paranormal investigation techniques have evolved significantly over the years, blending traditional methods with modern technology to enhance the quest for understanding the supernatural. One notable technique is the use of Electronic Voice Phenomena (EVP) recording. Investigators utilize audio equipment to capture voices or sounds that are not audible to the human ear during a session. This method involves asking questions and allowing for silence, during which spirits may communicate through vibrations that the equipment can pick up. The analysis of these recordings has led to many chilling revelations and remains a staple in ghost hunting.

Another technique gaining popularity among paranormal enthusiasts is the use of thermal imaging cameras. These devices detect temperature variations in an environment, which can indicate the presence of a spirit. Cold spots, often associated with ghostly activity, can be visualized through thermal imaging, allowing investigators to pinpoint areas of interest. When combined with other methods, such as EVP sessions or medium assessments, thermal imaging provides a more comprehensive picture of a location's paranormal activity.

In addition to technology, the use of dowsing rods has persisted as a traditional method for locating spiritual energy or communicating with spirits. Many investigators employ these simple tools, typically made of metal, to find ley lines or energy sources in a location. The rods move in response to unseen forces, guiding the investigator to points of interest where spiritual activity may be heightened. This technique often appeals to those who favor a more intuitive approach to paranormal investigations.

Spirit boxes, or ghost boxes, represent yet another innovative method for communication with the other side. These devices scan through radio frequencies, creating a white noise effect that spirits can allegedly manipulate to form words or sentences. Paranormal enthusiasts often report strikingly clear and relevant messages received through spirit boxes, leading to compelling evidence of communication. This technique has sparked fascination and debate within the community, as enthusiasts strive to discern genuine messages from random noise.

Lastly, the practice of historical research plays a crucial role in paranormal investigations, especially regarding historical hauntings. Understanding the background of a location, including significant events, past inhabitants, and local legends, can provide context to the paranormal phenomena experienced. By weaving together historical narratives with investigative techniques, enthusiasts can form a more complete understanding of the spirit world, allowing them to engage with both the past and the supernatural in meaningful ways. This holistic approach enriches the investigation experience, attracting those passionate about ghost stories, urban legends, and the exploration of haunted histories.

Case Studies of Famous Investigations

The realm of paranormal investigations is rich with case studies that captivate enthusiasts and scholars alike. Among the most renowned is the investigation of the Amityville Horror, which began in 1975 when the Lutz family moved into a house where a gruesome mass murder had occurred. The family's experiences, which included strange noises, cold spots, and apparitions, ignited public fascination and skepticism. The Lutzes' claims were investigated by Ed and Lorraine Warren, prominent paranormal investigators, who reported a heavy, oppressive atmosphere and various supernatural occurrences. This case not only sparked a media frenzy but also raised questions about the nature of hauntings and the interplay between trauma, memory, and the paranormal.

Another compelling investigation is the Enfield Poltergeist case, which took place in England during the late 1970s. The Hodgson family reported a series of bizarre incidents, including furniture moving on its own and strange noises. Investigators, including paranormal researchers Maurice Grosse and Guy Lyon Playfair, documented the events and conducted interviews with the family. The case gained notoriety due to the alleged possession of one of the daughters, Janet, who exhibited behaviors that many considered to be beyond the realm of normal human experience. This investigation highlighted the complexities of poltergeist phenomena and the psychological implications of such experiences, drawing attention from both skeptics and believers.

The haunting of the Winchester Mystery House in California presents a fascinating case of historical significance intertwined with paranormal elements. Built by Sarah Winchester, the widow of gun magnate William Wirt Winchester, the sprawling mansion is famous for its architectural oddities and continuous construction. Legend holds that Sarah believed she was haunted by the spirits of those killed by Winchester rifles and that building the house would appease them. Paranormal investigations at the site have reported ghostly manifestations, unexplained noises, and a feeling of being watched. This case illustrates the profound connection between personal grief, historical context, and spectral encounters, making it a staple in discussions about hauntings.

The Bell Witch haunting, which occurred in the early 19th century in Tennessee, is another significant case that has become embedded in American folklore. The Bell family reported disturbances ranging from strange noises to physical attacks, prompting local interest and investigations. One of the most notable aspects of this case is the alleged interaction between the family and an entity known as the Bell Witch, who claimed to be the spirit of a woman named Kate Batts. The events surrounding the Bell Witch sparked debates about folklore, superstition, and the societal implications of hauntings, ultimately influencing literature and popular culture.

Lastly, the investigation of the Stanley Hotel, famously linked to Stephen King's "The Shining," showcases the intersection of literary inspiration and real-life hauntings. Guests and staff have reported numerous ghostly encounters, including sightings of the hotel's founder, F.O. Stanley. Paranormal investigations have consistently revealed unexplained phenomena, making the hotel a popular destination for ghost hunters. This case emphasizes how historical narratives, personal experiences, and cultural references shape our understanding of hauntings, inviting both skepticism and intrigue within the paranormal community. Each of these investigations offers unique insights into the phenomenon of hauntings, intertwining history, psychology, and the supernatural in ways that continue to fascinate and provoke thought among those drawn to the mysteries of the past.

5

Ghost Hunting Equipment Reviews

Essential Ghost Hunting Tools

In the realm of ghost hunting, having the right tools can significantly enhance the experience and increase the likelihood of encountering the supernatural. Essential ghost hunting tools are designed to help enthusiasts detect, measure, and communicate with spirits. These devices range from basic, easily accessible items to more advanced technology, each serving a unique purpose in the investigation process.

One of the most fundamental tools is the EMF meter, which detects electromagnetic fields that are often associated with paranormal activity. Ghost hunters believe that spirits can create disturbances in the electromagnetic field, leading to fluctuations that can be recorded with this device. EMF meters come in various forms, from simple handheld models to more sophisticated versions with data logging capabilities. By monitoring EMF levels in a location, investigators can identify hotspots where spirit activity is more likely to occur, guiding them in their search for evidence.

Another important tool is the digital voice recorder, used for capturing electronic voice phenomena (EVPs). These are unexplained sounds or voices that some believe are communications from spirits. A digital voice recorder allows for high-quality audio capture, essential for later analysis. Ghost hunters often conduct sessions where they ask questions to the unseen entities and then review the recordings to identify any anomalous responses. The methodical documentation of these findings can contribute to understanding the history and character of the hauntings being investigated.

In addition to these devices, thermal imaging cameras have gained popularity among paranormal investigators. These cameras detect heat signatures, allowing hunters to visualize temperature fluctuations that might indicate the presence of a spirit. Cold spots, which are often reported in haunted locations, can be identified through thermal imaging, providing a visual representation of potential paranormal activity. The ability to see these temperature changes can enhance the investigation, offering physical evidence of unexplained phenomena that might otherwise go unnoticed.

Finally, ghost hunters often equip themselves with tools for spiritual communication, such as pendulums or spirit boards. These instruments are rooted in spiritualism and are used to facilitate contact with the spirit world. While their effectiveness may vary among practitioners, many ghost enthusiasts report intriguing experiences when using these tools during investigations. The combination of technology and traditional spiritual practices allows for a more holistic approach to uncovering the mysteries of hauntings, bridging the gap between historical narratives and modern paranormal experiences.

By utilizing a diverse array of ghost hunting tools, enthusiasts can engage with the haunting narratives that permeate our history. Each device serves to illuminate the unseen, offering a glimpse into the stories and legends that shape our understanding of the paranormal. Whether it's the cold whisper of a ghostly presence or the flicker of an EMF meter, these tools enable a deeper exploration of the shadows that linger from the past, inviting both seasoned investigators and curious newcomers to participate in the ongoing dialogue between the living and the dead.

New Technologies in Ghost Hunting

The field of ghost hunting has evolved significantly over the years, especially with the advent of new technologies that enhance the ways enthusiasts investigate paranormal phenomena. Traditional ghost hunting methods, such as using pendulums or Ouija boards, have gradually been supplemented by a range of innovative devices that offer more precise data and insights. These technologies not only provide a means to capture evidence of ghostly presences but also contribute to a more systematic approach to ghost investigations. As paranormal enthusiasts delve deeper into the mysteries of hauntings, embracing these advancements can lead to richer experiences and potentially clearer encounters with the unknown.

One of the most significant advancements in ghost hunting technology is the introduction of digital voice recorders and audio analysis software. EVP (Electronic Voice Phenomena) sessions have become a staple in paranormal investigations, allowing ghost hunters to capture voices that are not audible during the recording. The ability to analyze these recordings using software that enhances audio quality or removes background noise has revolutionized how investigators interpret their findings. Enthusiasts can now sift through hours of recordings, identifying potential ghostly communications that might have been missed in the past, thus adding credibility to their claims of hauntings.

Additionally, the use of infrared cameras and thermal imaging devices has transformed the visual aspect of ghost hunting. These technologies enable investigators to see heat signatures and detect changes in temperature, which can indicate the presence of a spirit. In historical locations known for their ghostly activity, such as old mansions or battlefields, these devices can provide compelling visual evidence that complements the auditory findings. The ability to document these anomalies with high-resolution images or videos further strengthens the case for the existence of paranormal entities, allowing enthusiasts to share their experiences with a broader audience.

Smartphone applications designed for ghost hunting have also surged in popularity. These apps utilize various sensors available in modern smartphones to detect electromagnetic fields, temperature fluctuations, and even spirit communication through random word generation. While these applications are often met with skepticism regarding their accuracy, many ghost hunters appreciate the convenience and accessibility they offer. The integration of technology into everyday devices allows a wider range of people to engage in ghost hunting, making it a more inclusive and community-driven activity. This shift not only expands the pool of potential investigators but also fosters a collaborative spirit among enthusiasts.

Finally, the rise of virtual reality (VR) and augmented reality (AR) technologies presents exciting new frontiers for paranormal investigation. These immersive experiences allow users to explore haunted locations from the comfort of their homes or enhance real-world explorations with digital overlays that provide historical context or highlight reported paranormal activity. As VR and AR technologies continue to advance, they could revolutionize the way ghost stories are told and experienced, bridging the gap between the supernatural and the tangible world. For paranormal enthusiasts, these innovations not only provide new ways to engage with history and legends but also deepen their understanding of the ghostly manifestations that persist in our collective consciousness.

Reviews of Popular Ghost Hunting Gear

In the realm of ghost hunting, the right equipment can significantly enhance the experience and success of paranormal investigations. Various tools have been developed over the years, each designed to detect, record, or interact with the supernatural. Among the most popular gear are EMF meters, which measure electromagnetic fields. These devices are often used by ghost hunters to identify unusual spikes in electromagnetic activity that could indicate the presence of a spirit. While many skeptics argue that these fluctuations can be attributed to electrical appliances, dedicated paranormal enthusiasts maintain that consistent readings in historically haunted locations may correlate with ghostly manifestations.

Another essential piece of equipment for ghost hunters is the digital voice recorder. These devices capture audio, enabling investigators to listen for Electronic Voice Phenomena (EVP)—unexplained voices or sounds that are believed to be communications from spirits. Many ghost hunters have reported capturing EVPs during investigations, leading to chilling revelations and unforgettable experiences. However, the interpretation of these recordings often requires a discerning ear, as background noise and environmental sounds can sometimes obscure genuine paranormal evidence. Thus, understanding how to use digital voice recorders effectively is crucial for any serious investigator.

Infrared cameras and night vision devices have also gained popularity among ghost hunters. These tools allow for visibility in complete darkness, which is especially valuable during nighttime investigations in reputedly haunted locations. Infrared cameras can capture images and video that might reveal shadowy figures or unexplained movements. Urban legends often emerge from footage taken with these devices, where viewers claim to see apparitions or orbs. While skeptics may dismiss this as mere trickery of light, the thrill of capturing something inexplicable drives many enthusiasts to employ these high-tech tools in their explorations.

Another notable piece of equipment is the spirit box, a device that scans radio frequencies to facilitate communication with spirits. Users of spirit boxes believe that entities can manipulate the radio waves to form words or phrases, allowing for a dialogue between the living and the deceased. This tool has gained a cult following among paranormal investigators, especially in locations with rich historical hauntings. While the validity of spirit box communications is often debated, many ghost hunters find the experience exhilarating, as it adds a layer of interaction to their investigations.

Lastly, paranormal enthusiasts often utilize ghost hunting apps available for smartphones. These apps range from EMF detectors to spirit communication tools, and while they may not have the same reliability as dedicated equipment, they offer an accessible entry point for newcomers to the field. With the rise of technology, these applications have sparked interest in ghost hunting among a wider audience, allowing people to explore the world of hauntings and urban legends with minimal investment. As the fascination with the paranormal continues to grow, ghost hunting gear remains a vital aspect of the adventure, empowering enthusiasts to delve deeper into the shadows of the past.

6 |

Celebrity Ghost Encounters

Famous Figures and Their Ghostly Encounters

Throughout history, numerous famous figures have reported ghostly encounters that blur the lines between the known and the supernatural. From writers to politicians, these experiences often reflect the fears, beliefs, and cultural contexts of their time. Famous encounters not only provide insight into the personal lives of these individuals but also contribute to the rich tapestry of ghost stories that have captivated audiences for centuries.

One of the most renowned figures associated with ghostly encounters is Charles Dickens. The celebrated author was known for his fascination with the supernatural, which is evident in his literary works. Dickens claimed to have had several ghostly experiences, including a notable encounter in his London home. He described hearing mysterious footsteps and feeling an otherworldly presence, which inspired his classic tale "A Christmas Carol." Dickens's belief in spirits and their influence on the living reflects the Victorian era's growing interest in spiritualism and the afterlife, making his experiences particularly significant in the context of historical hauntings.

Another prominent figure with a ghostly story is President Abraham Lincoln. It is said that Lincoln had a keen interest in the paranormal, frequently attending séances and engaging with spiritualists to communicate with the dead. His encounters are often recounted, particularly the night he visited a séance hosted by a famous medium, where he reportedly saw the spirit of his deceased son, Willie. Lincoln's experiences not only illustrate his personal grief but also highlight the era's fascination with the afterlife and the connections between the living and the dead, making his story a compelling part of American folklore.

In the realm of literature, authors like Edgar Allan Poe and Mark Twain have also shared eerie encounters. Poe, known for his macabre tales, often found inspiration in the supernatural. He reportedly claimed to have been visited by the ghost of a lost love, which influenced his writing style and themes of longing and loss. Meanwhile, Twain's experiences included an unsettling encounter in a haunted hotel, where he described witnessing ghostly apparitions that left a lasting impression on his literary works. Both authors contribute to the understanding of how ghostly manifestations can seep into literature, enriching their stories and connecting readers with the spectral realm.

Lastly, one cannot overlook the accounts of modern celebrities who have encountered spirits. Figures such as actress Whoopi Goldberg and singer Taylor Swift have spoken openly about their experiences with ghosts. Goldberg, in particular, has detailed her interactions with the spirit world through her work in the film "Ghost" and her personal encounters, influencing public perception of ghosts in contemporary culture. Swift has mentioned feeling the presence of spirits in her historic homes, blending her artistry with the echoes of past inhabitants. These modern encounters continue to spark interest in ghost stories, illustrating that the fascination with the paranormal transcends time and remains relevant in popular culture today.

How Celebrity Experiences Shape Public Perception

Celebrity experiences with the paranormal often serve as powerful catalysts in shaping public perception of ghostly phenomena. When well-known figures share their encounters with the supernatural, they lend a certain legitimacy to the experiences that might otherwise be dismissed. This phenomenon can be traced back to historical instances where celebrities have engaged with ghostly lore, such as the spiritualist movements of the 19th century. Figures like Arthur Conan Doyle, creator of Sherlock Holmes, were vocal proponents of spiritualism, and their endorsements helped propel the movement into the mainstream, influencing a generation's understanding of the afterlife and the existence of spirits.

Media portrayals of celebrity ghost encounters contribute significantly to the public's fascination with the paranormal. Television shows, documentaries, and reality series often feature celebrities recounting their eerie experiences in haunted locations. Such presentations not only entertain but also create a narrative that intertwines celebrity culture with the paranormal. For example, when a famous actor visits a reputedly haunted site and shares their unsettling experience, it can spark widespread interest in the location itself. Fans may flock to these sites, hoping to encounter the same phenomena that captured their idol's attention, thus further embedding the location in the cultural consciousness.

Moreover, the impact of social media cannot be overlooked in this context. Celebrities sharing their ghostly encounters on platforms like Instagram or Twitter can generate immediate and widespread discussion. These posts often lead to a viral effect, where the narrative of the haunting is shared, commented on, and dissected by fans and skeptics alike. This rapid dissemination of information shapes perceptions not only of the celebrity involved but also of the paranormal itself. The casual mention of a ghostly encounter by a beloved celebrity can transform public understanding and acceptance of hauntings, moving them from the realm of folklore to a more accepted reality in the eyes of many.

The interplay between celebrity and the paranormal is also evident in the growing interest in ghost hunting and paranormal investigation. As celebrities engage in these activities, whether through television shows or personal endeavors, they inspire their fans to explore similar paths. This influence can lead to the rise of amateur ghost hunters, equipped with the latest ghost hunting equipment and armed with a newfound enthusiasm for uncovering the mysteries of the supernatural. The celebrity endorsement of such activities fosters a community of like-minded individuals who share tips, experiences, and equipment reviews, thereby creating a robust subculture centered around the exploration of hauntings and ghostly manifestations.

Finally, the portrayal of celebrity ghost encounters in literature further complicates public perceptions of the paranormal. Books that document these experiences often mix personal anecdotes with historical context, allowing readers to engage with the material on multiple levels. They can find themselves drawn into the narratives crafted by their favorite celebrities while simultaneously learning about the historical hauntings that inspired these tales. This fusion of personal experience and historical narrative serves to deepen the intrigue surrounding the paranormal, encouraging a more nuanced understanding of how these experiences can shape both individual beliefs and collective cultural narratives about the afterlife and the existence of spirits.

Media Representation of Celebrity Hauntings

Media representation of celebrity hauntings plays a significant role in shaping public perception of both the supernatural and the celebrities involved. In recent years, the coupling of fame with the paranormal has led to a unique intersection where ghost stories and celebrity culture merge. This phenomenon not only captivates audiences but also encourages them to explore the historical and cultural contexts of hauntings. Through television shows, documentaries, podcasts, and social media, stories of celebrity ghost encounters gain traction, often becoming urban legends in their own right, further blurring the lines between fact and fiction.

Television networks have capitalized on the allure of celebrity hauntings by producing reality shows that focus on the paranormal experiences of famous individuals. Programs like "Celebrity Ghost Stories" invite well-known personalities to share their eerie encounters, providing an intimate glimpse into their encounters with the supernatural. These narratives often include dramatic reenactments, which enhance the storytelling aspect, drawing viewers into the emotional and psychological experiences of the celebrities. Consequently, these portrayals not only serve to entertain but also to validate the experiences of those who have encountered hauntings, creating a sense of community among paranormal enthusiasts.

Social media platforms have further amplified the reach and impact of celebrity hauntings. Influencers and fans alike share stories and theories about famous figures haunted by their pasts, crafting a digital folklore that engages a global audience. Hashtags and viral posts create a sense of immediacy that traditional media cannot match, allowing for real-time discussions and analyses of ghostly encounters. This participatory culture encourages viewers to investigate the historical backgrounds of the haunted locations, fostering a deeper understanding of the interplay between celebrity culture and the paranormal.

The influence of literature on the portrayal of celebrity hauntings cannot be overlooked. Authors often weave ghostly narratives around famous figures, enriching the lore surrounding their lives and deaths. These literary interpretations explore themes of regret, unfinished business, and the persistent nature of fame beyond the grave. Ghostly manifestations in literature serve as a canvas for examining societal views on mortality, legacy, and the supernatural. By analyzing these stories, paranormal enthusiasts gain insight into the cultural anxieties and aspirations that shape our understanding of hauntings.

Celebrity hauntings also invite a critical examination of spiritualism and mediumship practices. As public figures engage with the paranormal, they often become conduits for broader discussions about the afterlife, grief, and the human experience. The exploration of celebrity ghost encounters can demystify spiritual practices, making them more accessible to the general public. This not only enriches the conversation surrounding hauntings but also fosters a greater appreciation for the complexities of life, death, and the possibility of communication with those who have passed. In this way, media representation of celebrity hauntings serves as a bridge between entertainment and the profound mysteries of existence.

7

Ghostly Manifestations in Literature

The Role of Ghosts in Classic Literature

The role of ghosts in classic literature serves as a fascinating reflection of societal fears, moral dilemmas, and cultural beliefs. From ancient texts to Victorian novels, the presence of spectral figures often signifies more than mere fright; they reveal the complexities of human existence and the unresolved issues that linger beyond death. In many classics, ghosts are not only harbingers of doom

but also messengers, guiding the living through their moral quandaries and unresolved pasts. This duality enhances the depth of the narratives, transforming spectral appearances into critical elements that drive the plot and character development.

In works such as Shakespeare's "Hamlet," the ghost of King Hamlet embodies themes of revenge and justice, compelling his son to confront moral and existential questions. The spectral visitation serves as a catalyst for action, pushing the protagonist into a spiral of introspection and conflict that ultimately leads to tragic consequences. Similarly, in Charles Dickens' "A Christmas Carol," the ghostly encounters of Ebenezer Scrooge illustrate the consequences of a life devoid of compassion and generosity. These apparitions not only haunt Scrooge but also offer him a chance at redemption, illustrating how ghosts can serve as instruments of moral reckoning within literature.

Classic literature also uses ghosts to explore themes of memory and trauma. In Henry James' "The Turn of the Screw," the ambiguous presence of the ghosts of Peter Quint and Miss Jessel raises questions about the reliability of perception and

the impact of past traumas on the present. The spectral figures become symbols of repressed memories, reflecting the psychological struggles of the characters and challenging readers to consider the thin line between reality and illusion. This exploration of the psyche through ghostly manifestations adds a layer of complexity to the narrative, inviting deeper analysis of the characters' motivations and fears.

Moreover, the fascination with ghosts in literature mirrors societal attitudes toward death and the afterlife. In the Gothic tradition, ghost stories often reveal cultural anxieties surrounding mortality, the unknown, and the supernatural. Authors like Mary Shelley and Edgar Allan Poe utilized spectral elements to delve into themes of loss, madness, and the consequences of defying natural laws. These ghostly narratives not only entertain but also serve as a means for society to confront its fears and grapple with the mysteries of existence, making them timeless and relevant across generations.

The enduring popularity of ghostly figures in classic literature has also paved the way for modern interpretations and adaptations, inspiring contemporary ghost stories and paranormal investigations. As a result, the legacy of these literary apparitions continues to resonate within the paranormal community, inviting enthusiasts to explore the historical and cultural contexts that shaped these narratives. In this way, ghosts in literature act as a bridge between the past and present, fostering a deeper understanding of human experiences and the mysteries that persist beyond the grave.

Modern Literature and Its Ghostly Themes

Modern literature has increasingly embraced ghostly themes, reflecting society's fascination with the supernatural and the unknown. Authors draw from historical hauntings and urban legends, weaving these elements into narratives that explore the human experience through the lens of the paranormal. This trend highlights not only a cultural obsession with ghosts but also a deeper inquiry into memory, loss, and the lingering impact of the past. The ghostly manifestations in contemporary literature often serve as metaphors for unresolved issues, societal fears, and the complexities of human relationships.

Many modern writers utilize ghosts to symbolize the haunting nature of personal and collective trauma. For instance, novels like "The Lovely Bones" by Alice Sebold explore the afterlife through the eyes of a murdered girl watching over her family. This narrative not only delves into the emotional turmoil of loss but also raises questions about justice, memory, and the connections that persist beyond death. Such stories resonate with readers who are drawn to the intersection of the living and the dead, illustrating how literature can provide a medium to confront uncomfortable truths and unresolved feelings.

The influence of historical hauntings is particularly evident in works that incorporate real-life events and figures into their narratives. Authors often blend fiction with documented hauntings, creating a tapestry that enriches the reading experience. For example, Sarah Waters' "The Little Stranger" intertwines the ghostly with the historical, set in a post-World War II England grappling with class and decay. Through this, readers encounter not just spectral experiences but also the societal shifts of the time, making the ghost a representative of historical forces that continue to shape the present.

Urban legends also play a significant role in modern literature's ghostly themes. These stories, often rooted in local folklore, provide a rich source of inspiration for writers seeking to evoke a sense of place and cultural identity. Works like "The Cabin at the End of the World" by Paul Tremblay illustrate how contemporary fears and anxieties are manifested through ghostly elements. By drawing on urban legends, authors tap into shared cultural narratives, allowing readers to engage with their own fears while exploring the boundaries between reality and the supernatural.

As interest in the paranormal grows, the intersection of literature and ghostly themes also finds expression in digital media, from podcasts to interactive storytelling. This evolution reflects a broader cultural shift toward embracing the unknown and the unexplained. Paranormal enthusiasts and ghost story fans are increasingly drawn to narratives that challenge their perceptions of reality, inviting them to explore the mysteries that lie just beyond the veil of the living world. Modern literature, with its ghostly themes, serves as a powerful reminder of the enduring presence of the past, urging us to confront what haunts us in both life and death.

Analyzing Ghosts as Literary Devices

Analyzing ghosts as literary devices reveals how they serve multifaceted roles in literature, often reflecting cultural anxieties and societal norms. Ghosts in literature are not merely spectral figures; rather, they symbolize unresolved issues, unfulfilled desires, and the haunting nature of the past. From Shakespeare's "Hamlet" to modern horror novels, ghosts often embody the emotional and psychological struggles of characters, acting as catalysts for conflict and transformation. As such, they invite readers to explore deeper themes of mortality, memory, and the consequences of actions long gone.

In historical contexts, ghosts frequently represent the collective memory of a society. They evoke the spirits of those who have suffered injustices, serving as reminders of unresolved conflicts or tragedies. For example, in many ghost stories, the apparitions of the deceased arise to seek justice or closure for their untimely deaths. This literary device not only entertains but also educates readers about historical events, encouraging them to ponder the implications of the past on the present. Such narratives often weave together the threads of personal and collective histories, illustrating how the echoes of bygone eras continue to shape contemporary life.

Urban legends frequently employ ghosts as central figures, using them to communicate moral lessons or cultural fears. These stories often emerge from specific settings, such as haunted houses or abandoned places, where the supernatural intertwines with the everyday. Through these narratives, ghosts embody the fears of urban life, including isolation, societal decay, and the loss of community. The haunting figures serve as metaphors for the darker aspects of modern existence, prompting readers to confront their own anxieties about the unknown and the unseen. This connection between ghosts and urban legends highlights their role as a reflection of societal issues that resonate with readers across generations.

Ghostly manifestations in literature also explore themes of spiritualism and the afterlife, delving into the human fascination with what lies beyond death. Many authors have drawn upon the spiritualist movement to portray ghosts as intermediaries between the living and the dead. This portrayal raises questions about the nature of existence and the possibility of life after death, inviting readers to consider their own beliefs and experiences with the paranormal. Such narratives often challenge the boundary between reality and the supernatural, encouraging a dialogue about the unseen forces that may influence human lives.

Ultimately, analyzing ghosts as literary devices enriches our understanding of literature and its capacity to reflect human experiences. Ghosts provide a lens through which we can examine not only personal fears and desires but also broader societal issues and historical injustices. In the realm of ghost stories, these spectral figures become powerful symbols that transcend their haunting nature, offering insights into the complexities of life, death, and the narratives that bind us to our past. For paranormal enthusiasts and ghost story fans, engaging with these literary ghosts enhances the appreciation of the genre, revealing the depth and significance behind every haunting tale.

8

Spiritualism and Mediumship Practices

The History of Spiritualism

The history of spiritualism is a fascinating journey that intertwines belief systems, societal changes, and the quest for understanding life beyond death. Emerging in the early 19th century in the United States, spiritualism was largely influenced by the desire to communicate with the deceased. The movement gained momentum through the experiences of the Fox sisters in Hydesville, New York, where alleged spirit manifestations, such as rapping sounds, captivated the public's imagination. This event marked the inception of a movement that sought to bridge the gap between the living and the spirit world, offering solace to those mourning lost loved ones.

As spiritualism spread across North America and Europe, it attracted a diverse following, including intellectuals, artists, and even prominent figures like Arthur Conan Doyle. The movement was characterized by public séances, where mediums performed demonstrations of their abilities to contact spirits. The rise of spiritualism coincided with the Industrial Revolution, a time when many faced rapid societal changes and existential questions. People turned to spiritualism as a means of coping with loss and uncertainty, seeking answers to profound questions about existence and the afterlife.

The spiritualist community developed a range of practices and beliefs that became integral to the movement. Mediumship, the practice of communicating with spirits, was central to spiritualist gatherings. Various techniques, including trance mediumship, table tipping, and the use of Ouija boards, became commonplace. These practices not only served as a form of entertainment but also reinforced the belief in a continuing connection between the living and the dead. The spiritualist movement also contributed to the development of ghost hunting as a serious pursuit, with enthusiasts seeking to document and understand paranormal phenomena.

However, the movement faced significant scrutiny and criticism. Many skeptics emerged, exposing fraudulent mediums and manipulating techniques that misled grieving individuals. Prominent figures like Harry Houdini dedicated their lives to debunking fraudulent practices, emphasizing the need for critical thinking and skepticism in the face of supernatural claims. Despite this backlash, spiritualism continued to evolve, adapting to the changing cultural landscape and maintaining a dedicated following.

By the mid-20th century, spiritualism experienced a resurgence, influenced by the New Age movement and renewed interest in the paranormal. This revival saw the integration of spiritualist principles into broader metaphysical practices, fostering a renewed belief in the possibility of communication with spirits. Today, spiritualism remains a vibrant part of paranormal culture, with a rich legacy that influences ghost stories, urban legends, and the ongoing fascination with hauntings. As enthusiasts continue to explore the depths of spiritualism, the echoes of the past resonate with a profound desire to understand the mysteries of life, death, and what lies beyond.

Techniques of Mediumship

Mediumship is an ancient practice that seeks to bridge the gap between the living and the deceased. Various techniques have been developed over the years, each harnessing unique abilities to facilitate communication with spirits. For paranormal enthusiasts, understanding these techniques not only enriches their experience but also enhances their ability to explore the supernatural realms. Among the most recognized methods are clairaudience, clairvoyance, and physical mediumship, each offering distinct avenues for connection with the spirit world.

Clairaudience, or clear hearing, allows mediums to receive messages from spirits through auditory means. This technique may manifest as distinct voices, whispers, or sounds that are perceptible only to the medium. Practitioners often report hearing specific phrases or even entire conversations that provide insight into the spirit's past or unresolved issues. Ghost story fans may find this technique particularly fascinating, as it aligns closely with many urban legends that involve spirits communicating through eerie sounds or voices, adding an auditory layer to haunted locations that can evoke intense emotional responses.

Clairvoyance, or clear seeing, enables mediums to visualize spirits and their environments. This often involves receiving images or impressions in the mind's eye, allowing the medium to convey messages about the spirit's life, personality, or circumstances surrounding their death. Historical hauntings frequently feature accounts where mediums have described scenes or events from the past, providing context to ghostly encounters. For paranormal investigators, honing clairvoyant skills can significantly enhance their ability to interpret phenomena during ghost hunts, leading to more profound connections with the spirits they seek to understand.

Physical mediumship encompasses a range of phenomena where the medium becomes a conduit for spirit manifestations. This might include the movement of objects, changes in temperature, or even the appearance of ectoplasm. These visceral experiences can profoundly impact those present, creating tangible evidence of the supernatural. Within the realm of celebrity ghost encounters, stories abound of famous mediums who have facilitated dramatic physical manifestations, captivating audiences and reinforcing the belief in the presence of spirits. Such accounts often serve to bridge the gap between entertainment and serious paranormal investigation.

Lastly, trance mediumship involves the medium entering a trance state, allowing a spirit to take control of their body and communicate directly. This technique can lead to powerful experiences, as the medium may deliver messages in the spirit's voice, sharing insights that resonate deeply with those seeking closure or understanding. In literature, depictions of trance mediumship often highlight the intense emotional exchanges between the living and the dead, showcasing the timeless quest for connection that defines the human experience. For ghost hunters and spiritualists alike, mastering this technique can be transformative, opening doors to profound revelations and deepening their understanding of the unseen world.

The Impact of Spiritualism on Ghost Encounters

The rise of Spiritualism in the 19th century significantly influenced the way ghost encounters were perceived and documented. Spiritualism, born out of a desire to communicate with the deceased, provided a framework through which individuals could interpret unexplained phenomena. This movement, which gained traction after the Fox sisters in New York claimed to communicate with spirits, opened the floodgates for countless ghost stories and encounters. As more people sought to understand the afterlife and connect with lost loved ones, the concept of hauntings shifted from superstition to a more accepted aspect of human experience.

The practice of mediumship became central to Spiritualism, presenting a new avenue for ghost encounters. Mediums, often celebrated figures in their communities, claimed to possess the ability to communicate with spirits. Their séances attracted both skeptics and believers, creating a cultural phenomenon where ghostly manifestations were not only reported but also ritualized. This legitimization of spirit communication led to a surge in ghost stories, as individuals began sharing their own experiences, seeking both solace and validation. Ghost encounters transformed into narratives that blended personal grief with spiritual exploration, reinforcing the belief that the dead could influence the living.

As Spiritualism spread, it also intersected with emerging scientific inquiries into the paranormal. The late 19th and early 20th centuries saw a burgeoning interest in spiritual phenomena from a scientific perspective. Researchers began to apply methods of observation and experimentation to ghostly encounters, attempting to determine the authenticity of reported experiences. This period also introduced various ghost hunting techniques that are still in use today, such as the use of ouija boards and automatic writing. The blending of Spiritualism with scientific curiosity expanded the scope of ghost investigations, fostering a culture that embraced both the mystical and the empirical.

The literary world was not immune to the influence of Spiritualism either. Many authors began incorporating themes of ghost encounters into their works, reflecting societal interests in the afterlife and the unknown. Classic ghost stories often featured protagonists who engaged with spirits, highlighting the tension between the living and the dead. These tales not only entertained but also served to explore deeper philosophical questions regarding mortality, existence, and the possibility of life beyond death. The impact of Spiritualism on literature created a rich tapestry of narratives that continue to resonate within the ghost story genre today.

In contemporary paranormal investigations, the legacy of Spiritualism remains evident. Modern ghost hunters often utilize equipment and techniques inspired by early Spiritualist practices, such as EVP (Electronic Voice Phenomena) recordings and spirit boxes. The quest for evidence of the afterlife persists, echoing the fervor of 19th-century Spiritualist gatherings. The ongoing fascination with ghost encounters, fueled by a blend of historical context and personal experience, underscores a collective desire to connect with the past and to understand the mysteries that lie beyond the veil of death. This enduring intrigue ensures that the impact of Spiritualism on ghost encounters will continue to shape the landscape of paranormal exploration.

9

The Future of Hauntings

Changing Perceptions of the Paranormal

The perception of the paranormal has undergone significant transformations throughout history, reflecting cultural shifts, technological advancements, and changing societal attitudes toward the unknown. In ancient times, the supernatural was often woven directly into the fabric of daily life, with spirits and deities believed to influence human affairs. Folklore and oral traditions flourished, as tales of hauntings and spectral encounters were passed down through generations. These narratives served not only as entertainment but also as moral lessons, cautioning against the consequences of actions that might disturb the natural order or offend the spirits of the deceased.

The Enlightenment era marked a pivotal turning point, as rational thought and scientific inquiry began to challenge previously held beliefs about the supernatural. Ghost stories, once considered a staple of cultural identity, were relegated to the realms of superstition and folklore. The rise of empiricism and skepticism led to a decline in serious discussions about hauntings and the paranormal, as the focus shifted toward observable phenomena and logical explanations. However, this skepticism did not eradicate interest in the supernatural; instead, it galvanized a counter-movement that sought to explore the mysteries of the afterlife through new lenses, including spiritualism and the burgeoning field of psychology.

In the late 19th and early 20th centuries, spiritualism gained popularity as a legitimate way to connect with the deceased, leading to a renewed interest in ghostly manifestations. Séances, mediumship, and the use of Ouija boards became common practices, attracting both believers and skeptics. This era saw the emergence of prominent figures such as the Fox Sisters and later, figures like Harry Houdini, who sought to debunk fraudulent mediums while simultaneously expressing fascination with the unknown. The interplay between belief and skepticism during this period laid the groundwork for modern paranormal investigations, where the quest for evidence of hauntings became a structured endeavor.

The late 20th century and early 21st century brought about a surge in paranormal enthusiasm, fueled by the advent of technology and media portrayals of ghost hunting. Television shows, documentaries, and online platforms have democratized access to paranormal exploration, allowing enthusiasts to participate in investigations and share their findings. The development of ghost hunting equipment, such as EMF meters and digital voice recorders, has transformed the way individuals approach the investigation of hauntings. This technological evolution has not only changed perceptions of the paranormal but has also created a community that thrives on shared experiences and collective storytelling.

Today, the changing perceptions of the paranormal continue to evolve, reflecting broader societal changes and advancements in understanding human psychology. Ghost stories are no longer merely tales of terror; they often explore themes of loss, memory, and the human condition. As the lines between skepticism and belief blur, paranormal enthusiasts find themselves engaging with historical hauntings and urban legends in ways that honor both the past and present. This ongoing dialogue between the known and the unknown invites a deeper exploration of what it means to be haunted, ultimately enriching our understanding of the human experience and our relationship with the mysteries that lie beyond the veil.

The Role of Technology in Future Investigations

The advancement of technology has profoundly influenced the field of paranormal investigations, providing enthusiasts with innovative tools that enhance their understanding of hauntings and unexplained phenomena. Modern equipment such as digital voice recorders, electromagnetic field (EMF) meters, and thermal imaging cameras have become staples in the toolkit of ghost hunters. These devices not only aid in capturing evidence but also enable investigators to document their findings with unprecedented clarity. In an age where skepticism often overshadows belief, reliable technology serves as a bridge, allowing investigators to present their evidence in a manner that is both compelling and scientifically grounded.

One of the most significant contributions of technology to paranormal investigations is the proliferation of digital recording devices. Ghost hunters can now utilize high-definition cameras and sensitive audio recorders to capture potential ghostly manifestations. Advanced software aids in the analysis of these recordings, allowing for the identification of anomalies that might elude the naked eye or ear. This digital age has also made it easier to share findings with a wider audience through social media and online platforms, fostering a community of enthusiasts who can exchange insights and experiences related to hauntings and ghost stories.

Moreover, the integration of mobile applications tailored for paranormal investigations has transformed the way enthusiasts engage with their surroundings. Apps designed to detect EMF fluctuations or record environmental changes can provide real-time data, enhancing the interaction between the investigator and the haunted location. These applications often incorporate user-friendly interfaces that allow both seasoned investigators and novices to participate in the exploration of the unknown. As technology continues to evolve, it opens doors for new methodologies in documenting and interpreting paranormal occurrences.

Incorporating technology into paranormal investigations also encourages a more rigorous approach to the field. As investigators adopt scientific methods, the line between folklore and factual evidence can become clearer. For instance, the application of spectral analysis to audio recordings of purported EVP (electronic voice phenomena) allows for the differentiation between natural sounds and potential ghostly messages. This scientific lens promotes a more systematic investigation of urban legends and historical hauntings, providing a framework for understanding the cultural significance and historical context behind these phenomena.

Looking ahead, the future of paranormal investigations will likely see even more sophisticated advancements in technology. Innovations such as artificial intelligence and machine learning could revolutionize the analysis of collected data, identifying patterns or anomalies that might go unnoticed by human investigators. As the paranormal community embraces these technological advancements, it will continue to explore the rich tapestry of ghostly encounters and historical hauntings, blending the realms of science and spirituality in the pursuit of understanding the mysteries that lurk in the shadows of our past.

The Evolution of Ghost Stories in Popular Culture

The evolution of ghost stories in popular culture reflects a deep-seated fascination with the supernatural and the unknown that has persisted throughout history. From ancient folklore to contemporary media, these narratives have served as mirrors to societal fears, beliefs, and the human experience. Ghost stories have transitioned from oral traditions, where tales were shared around campfires, to printed literature, stage performances, and eventually digital platforms. Each form has contributed to the texture of ghostly narratives, shaping how they are perceived and understood by audiences.

In the 19th century, the rise of spiritualism marked a significant turning point in the portrayal of ghost stories. This movement, which emphasized communication with the dead through mediums, found its way into the hearts and homes of many. Ghost stories began to intertwine with the spiritualist beliefs of the time, as people sought to connect with lost loved ones. This period saw the emergence of classic ghost literature, with authors like Charles Dickens and Henry James crafting tales that explored the boundaries of life and death. The haunting in Dickens' "A Christmas Carol" and the eerie atmosphere of James' "The Turn of the Screw" exemplify how ghostly figures were used to comment on moral and societal issues.

The advent of the 20th century brought new technologies and mediums, which transformed how ghost stories were told. Film and radio allowed for a wider dissemination of ghostly tales, bringing chilling narratives into homes across the globe. The horror genre in cinema, particularly with classics like "The Haunting" and "The Shining," contributed to the popularization of ghost stories, portraying hauntings as not just physical manifestations but psychological explorations of fear and trauma. These adaptations often emphasized the psychological aspects of hauntings, resonating with audiences who sought deeper meanings behind the apparitions.

As urban legends emerged in tandem with growing urbanization, ghost stories began to reflect contemporary anxieties about modern life. The rise of the internet in the late 20th century provided a new platform for these narratives, where user-generated content and social media enabled the rapid sharing and evolution of ghost stories. Websites dedicated to urban legends and paranormal investigations allowed enthusiasts to engage with these tales in a communal setting, fostering a sense of shared experience. Ghost hunting shows and documentaries further fueled interest, transforming the act of storytelling into an active pursuit, where fans could participate in the search for the supernatural.

Today, ghost stories continue to thrive in popular culture, adapting to new societal contexts and technological advancements. From literature to video games, the themes of hauntings and the paranormal have found new life, captivating audiences with fresh interpretations. Celebrity ghost encounters and reality shows have introduced a new dimension to ghost stories, blending personal experiences with entertainment. As the boundaries between fact and fiction blur, the evolution of ghost stories remains a testament to humanity's enduring curiosity about the afterlife and the mysteries that lurk in the shadows of our past.